LETTER FROM A DISTANT LAND

1956 Lamont Poetry Selection

LETTER FROM A DISTANT LAND

BY

Philip Booth

NEW YORK

THE VIKING PRESS

1957

For
Margaret

ACKNOWLEDGMENT

Acknowledgment is made to the magazines in which a number of these poems were originally published: *The Atlantic Monthly, Audience, Beloit Poetry Journal, Harper's Bazaar, Hudson Review, Listen, The London Magazine, New Orleans Poetry Journal, The New Republic, The New Yorker, The Paris Review, Partisan Review, Poetry, The Saturday Review, The Sewanee Review, The Yale Review;* and to *Discovery, New World Writing,* and *New Poems by American Poets.*

CONTENTS

I

II

LETTER FROM A DISTANT LAND

I

looked down on through the ending rain,
divides to field and forest. Blurred
where first sun lifts the nimbus hung
in valleys, sharp with spruce ridged blue
across the mountains' granite spine,

this rooted plot of intervals,
green music from one morning word,
lies fallow still: as if men new
to gravity had not yet sprung
to claim these dark unsettled hills

or cultivate the wind-grazed meadows
Seen from this height, such deep woods fence
the unmown squares of sun that man
might seem unable, here, to clear
a long view from the tangled shadows.

Yet who will homestead here, shall count
his generation by the dense-
ringed stumps; as his seeds reach to bear,
he will in his first yield kneel down,
rooted where his praises mount.

GREAT FARM

In April, when raining is sunlight,
when dawn is a coarse young crow,
as willows bend to feather
the Great Farm springs to grow.

The orchard is loud: bees
and blossoms claim the bough;
a meadow of frogs, a sky
of swallows, flood the air now.

Two girls ride two white horses
(the world is green to plow!)
and sideways a big man with buckets
sets hugely to milk a big cow.

Long before October cold
touched frost to this high orchardrow
and burned the unpicked apples gold,

before the August boughs bent low
with Winesap weights; even before
the blossom stems began to grow

to fruit; while still the hidden store
of nectar held a summer hum
of hornets near the budding core;

when petaled June had not yet come
to earth in drifts around the root:
even then my good green thumb

had seeded centuries of loot,
and I, a vernal Adam, told
Eve when she should find the fruit.

The year is round around me now:
groundhog, mouse, and mole climb out,
blind and numb beside their burrow.

Worm and hornet, frog and hornpout,
surface from their sleeping mud.
Soft as pussywillows sprout,

barncats stretch and kittens bud.
This tidal circle spins me now
and greens my heart at April flood:

the chickadee, the winter sparrow,
blow North to Canada to breed;
a wet snail climbs the new-turned furrow.

A rash of robins land to feed;
pigweed, pokeweed, ragwort, mallow,
spring from summer's drifted seed.

The dogtooth steeps deep yellow
in deep shade. Dandelions sun
the lawn, last week's ponds are shallow.

The knotted grass snake is undone,
and warmer blood expands to know
the vernal course brown conies run.

[18]

The year is round around me now:
as I walk, turn, behind the harrow,
my feet take root against tomorrow.

Time was the apple Adam ate.
Eve bit, gave seconds to his mouth,
and then they had no minute left
to lose. Eyes opened in mid-kiss,
they saw, for once, raw nakedness,
and hid that sudden consequence
behind an hour's stripped leaves.

This is one sequence in the plot,
the garden where God came, that time,
to call. Hands behind him, walking
to and fro, he counted how
the fruit fell, bruised on frozen sod.
This was his orchard, his to pace;
the day was cool, and he was God.

Old Adam heard him humming, talking
to himself: *Winesap, King,*
           ripen in sun,
           McIntosh and
           Northern Spy
           fall one by one,
           ripen to die.

Adam heard him call his name,
but Adam, no old philosopher,
was not sure what he was after.
We're naked, Lord, and can't come out.

Eve nudged him with the bitter fruit.
God paused. *How do you know? Where is
that woman that I sprung from you?*

Eve held the twisted stem, the pulp;
she heard the low snake hiss, and let fly
blindly with a woman arm, careless
where her new-won anger struck.
The fodder for that two-fold flock
fell, an old brown core, at God's
stopped feet. He reached, and wound the clock.

While crabapple now is a windfall
of blossoms, why wait for a harvest
of worms? The wilding will shrivel
and sour this clearing, frost
will bite hard, and the crop
be lost.

But under woodpecker knock
in this rabbitrun wood, in May,
a sweet fern questionmark
whorls green as green is today,
and ferns ask no answer a swallow
can't fly.

When time is a troutlily yellow
as sun, what wildflowers weather
the high noon tomorrow?
Now jack-in-the-pulpits wither
for shade and there's maidenhair fern
to gather.

Now blossom is bloodroot is sap-run
is Spring, and true as arbutus
we're new. Words are a ruin
no animals heed, so kiss
me to silence: this wood
is for you.

NIGHTSONG

Beside you,
lying down at dark,
my waking fits your sleep.

Your turning
flares the slow-banked fire
between our mingled feet,

and there,
curved close and warm
against the nape of love,

held there,
who holds your dreaming
shape, I match my breathing

to your breath;
and sightlcss, keep my hand
on your heart's breast, keep

nightwatch
on your sleep to prove
there is no dark, nor death.

This side of silence,
where I hear my heartbeat
bump and balance
on the edge of sleep,

this side of silence
where my failing prayers
do awkward violence
to the dark, I keep

counting cadence,
numbering the quick
sequential sheep
that fold across the fence

of easy praise.
The wether's judas bell
leads them to leap,
and as they leap, betrays

the shepherd. He
walks watch where my uneven
pulse petitions sleep;
my name is Peter. I

promise, bless,
promise, yet I am like
a pelican
of the wilderness:

this side of silence
I deny myself,
begging balance
on this pasture rock;

this side of silence
I count the panicked lambs,
lambs that dance
within the scattered flock,

I pray me chance
for one hour's sleep, before
I hear the violence
of the cock.

Denial has a raucous voice: a black cock
racks the dawn, betrayal's bitter air
invades gray porches where the elders mock.
Men hammer crosses in the courthouse square.
Quick spit and stones accuse integrity.
Suspicion is a witness. Charges lodged
with kisses are on public trial, and he
who pleads his teaching is already judged.
Who lugs his freedom uphill in this year
will sweat with silent eloquence. His loss
is sentence in the noisy courts of fear,
memorial blood as on the bright-nailed Cross,
the lesson where our calendar began.
To spike a rumor, sacrifice a man.

SUNDAY CLIMB

Over Holt's Ledge
the riding hawk slides down a ridge
of air; the hillwind blinds my tears
to his far flight, but the hunter's course
he cruises my mind's eye can see
down mountainside topography.

Set under me
in Spring relief, the green-mapped valley
tilts with every wing-banked turn:
the flyway, wood, and chicken run
are hawks' fair game from this blue height,
and none escape my hawk's high sight.

His knife wings part
the Northern air in neither sport
nor hate: he climbs the thermals, rides
downwind, as only his tightening
entrails ache. I barely escape
wishing myself a hawk's pure shape,

but under the stoop
of those talons my rabbit hope
lies small against the ledge. And I
climb both as killer and as prey:
twice alone on the last height,
the sheer edge of human sight.

Under hawk-watch
over the river,
quick-schooled minnows
riffle the shallow
where I wade.

Fingerlings rise
in the pooled jade
at amber flies,
but only
fish-hawk hover
or kingfisher eye
can see below
the current-run
and river-race
to the legend
lying dark
in slow-finned grace.

And I, who lost
the rainbow risen
in the torrent
of my need,
cast and cast
again where he
lies deep while
his torn gills bleed.

And the dreamer hawk
high over that pool
in the streaming air
cries high and cool.

INSTRUCTION IN THE ART

"Take a boy fishing"

Boy, the giant beauty
that you cast for lies
upstream in this same current
that you wade. Men wise
with love have wintered
on the iron bridge, dreamed
opening day, and tied
their hatful of bright
artificial flies.

This is an old one, boy,
not in memory struck
at a false cast. No, nor
felt the quick-set hook.
The snags are ragged
with lost lures, hair and
gold; even icons shaped
like a woman, this beauty
never took.

Boy, cast lightly. Long
and lightly where the shallow
split tongue of current
undercuts the meadow;
in that spun pool

where blue flowers overhang
the bank, by first light
a few quiet men at last
have seen the shadow.

We only guess, boy,
by the stream-run shape
of steelheads, or a rainbow
beached in winter sleep.
Such forms lose color
in the creel; men file
barbs not toward food
or trophies, but for luck
they cannot keep.

Boy, the giant beauty
that you cast for lies
upstream. I pray you patience
for that tug and rise,
the risen image
that outleaps the rapids
in one illimitable
arc: to praise,
but not to prize.

II

THE LOST BOY

Tethered to no visible string, hung
    from nothing, yet swung
back and across the suburban river in almost
rhythmic arcs, the big red helicopter lurches
over the marsh edge, dips as it searches
    not for exotic prey,
but only for the local small boy
who went exploring and found himself lost.

Reported eight years old and six hours gone
    after sunfish, alone,
and wearing blue shorts, the boy knew how to swim.
Still, in the buggy dusk, his awkward parents thrash
their love against the thickets, the marsh
    holds a traffic
of volunteers who peer for his track,
and a red machine churns the air above him.

Around him, where he saw the spotted turtle
    sleep in sun, frogs startle
him from hunger. His rod (his father's) lies
cast aside downstream, the snagged line drawn taut,
too strong to break. Left weak and hot
    on his willowy patch
of flatland loud with wings, he turns to watch
the iridescent joining of blue dragonflies.

[35]

Whirring, tail tipped up, the male hovers
        over his mate, discovers
her, and parts with her in double flight.
Nothing the boy knows here but is unknown:
the lost rod, the long way home, the flown
        insects, and now
where it settles crabwise and slips low,
a red whirlybird flailing in the yellow light.

Its rotors squall the river where it swings
        crosswind, quiets, and hangs
with four bug legs poised above the found boy.
Tomorrow, the recess hero in a Monday school,
come late, he will be able to tell
        the sequence, play the airman
who hauled him aloft, and shape his airborne
hands to fly like the improbable whirling toy.

As he grows to solo through his heightened dreams
        he will try new terms
for flight, learn to armor words, design
ways to capture love, fish, and the world's spun map;
but now he spirals up toward sleep
        with no adequate speech
for exploration, and over him stretch
altitudes which he alone will define.

His father's sternness vibrates in his ear
        like the uneven roar
of mechanical rotors, and in his blurred eyes,

pulled to focus further than his mind can reach,
big red helicopters lurch
      rhythmically over
the bedposts; dance, climb, and hover,
paired with the persistent dragonflies.

When I was on Night Line,
flying my hands to park
a big-bird B-29,
I used to command the dark:
four engines were mine

to jazz; I was ground-crew,
an unfledged pfc,
but when I waved planes through
that flight line in Tennessee,
my yonder was wild blue.

Warming up, I was hot
on the throttle, logging an hour
of combat, I was the pilot
who rogered the tower.
I used to take off a lot.

With a flat-hat for furlough
and tin wings to sleep on,
I fueled my high-octane ego:
I buzzed, I landed my jeep on
the ramp, I flew low.

When a cross-country hop
let down, I was the big deal
who signaled big wheels to stop.
That's how I used to feel.
I used to get all revved up.

Come to conquer
this living labyrinth of rock,
    young Theseus of Dubuque
finds he is mazed without a minotaur,
without his Ariadne in the dark.

He dreams beyond
his steelwalled fear to fields grown
    vertical with corn
and hope. Home to this heroic end:
imprisoned in the city of alone;

here smog obscures
his visionary victor's world
    and streetsounds dulled
with rain reverberate in airshaft hours
where braver conquerors have been felled.

Amazed at night,
stalking the seven maids no sword
    can save, he is devoured
in passageways of reinforced concrete,
trapped by his beast, and overpowered

in sleepless dead-
end dreams. How now, Theseus? How send
    word home you are confined
with neither wings nor lover's thread
in the city that a murderer designed?

[40]

Strange, our not knowing
why the nighthawk lay still,

crouched on that high roof
where camouflage was cool.

We should have known. You proved
with the toss of a pebble

it was not death that turned
those eyes to chips of opal,

unlikely jewels folded
in an old paisley shawl.

Patience sheltered the bird
like dusk. Then the rung bell

tolled her fear to wing,
and we rose then, until,

made separate, we saw
the mottled egg left small:

an unprotected symbol;
warm, fragile, whole.

Hawk free of jess,
the diver springs
toward fire no son can bear,
arcs instantly,
and forms his highdive fall
against the incandescent air
still stressed with his lost wings.

His nerve-ends guess
brave distances
of space, but his sunstruck
timing fails:
he overreaches, swans,
and bellyflops in luck
gone bad in all grave instances.

New Aegeans press
their welcome over him:
his deepening flight
downs him
in green spectra where the sun
is drowned; phosphorescence lights
the treasure of his oceanic whim,

but in a wilderness
of eelgrass, kelp,
and shell, his breath is spent

imagining
that lanternfish are stars.
Unfound in this third element,
he fathoms down beyond all help

while every Daedalus
schemes on to soar.
Where discovery is to drown
he sounds
the whaling sea—this son
with sculpin, coin, and bone,
become the dark he must explore.

In praise of the redemptive rain stand bare
as birth, pray to the lightning, and naked-new,
sing thunder to the storming summer air.

Only with stripped senses and torrential prayer
can you, like one the whirlwind answers to,
in praise of the redemptive rain stand bare.

Be buffeted like preying hawks who dare
wild updrafts of desire: then can you
sing thunder to the storming summer air.

Like gamboling porpoises at sea, forswear
fool's shelter, foliage, or family pew.
In praise of the redemptive rain stand bare,

stand open as a wound. Unbound, declare
your weather-rage as ranging ospreys do:
sing thunder to the storming summer air.

Be healed in wash of water-fall, in tear
of wind. And where lightning strikes light through,
in praise of the redemptive rain stand bare,
sing thunder to the storming summer air.

SIASCONSET SONG

The girls
of golden summers whirl
through sunsprung
bright Julys
with born right
sky-bright
star-night
eyes;

everywhere
their tennis-twirl
of young gold
legs and arms,
they singsong
summer-long
I-belong
charms;

and through
the summer sailing swirl
they cut like
shining knives
in sun-told
never old
ever gold
lives.

SHAG

Under the slow heron,
flip tern, and swung gull,
six black shags run on
the water, each duck skull

filled with weathervane
thought. Toward east wind
they take off on the run,
splashing until the shag mind

tells spent feet to retract.
Then the seventh shag,
straggling, begins to react.
His head bobs. The fog

closing in, he raises
himself on gargoyle wings,
drops again, then rises
and runs as he bangs

the sea on all fours.
Slowly, then faster, he skims
the dark fir shores.
Momentarily, he seems

to join the first flight.
But he shoots away,
shag-like, his thought flat
black. All shags fly

low. Ornithologists know
more: the perhaps why
and improbable how
of shag flight. They

call them cormorants,
or latinize the North name.
I row slow in the dense
weather. This is Maine;

and I slap the split port oar
of my leaking skiff,
drifting among the fir
islands, the seabirds, as if

on vacation from knowledge:
six black shags, shagging;
August fog, me, a Maine ledge,
and the seventh shag, lagging.

IDENTIFICATION

Which is the tern?
  Those sea wings flung
  downwind, the torn
  cry, or the bird hung
  hovering to dive?

Or there, the fold
  of wing, the alive
  surprise held billed
  by the diver! Prove
  that is a tern.

All terns are small
  for fishers: black down
  caps, a forked tail,
  a snowsquall turn
  of breast, a dive.

But proof? No bird
  on the wind can prove
  flight with a word,
  nor do herring school
  through a sea of names.

The fish survive
  below surface storms
  and a bird can live
  nameless who swims
  with dry wings.

He digests the sea,
    his bright cry hangs
    on the wind; the prey
    of his dive rings
    a wing-split wave.

Curved windy-free,
    his flip wings prove
    the name, and his sea-
    cry dive like love,
    flung down the sky.

CHART 1203

Penobscot Bay and Approaches

Whoever works a storm to windward, sails
in rain, or navigates in island fog,
must reckon from the slow swung lead, from squalls

on cheek; must bear by compass, chart, and log.
Parallels are ruled from compass rose
to known red nun: but still the landfall leg

risks set of tide, lost buoys, and breakers' noise
on shore where no shore was. Whoever plots
his homing on these Eastward islands knows

how Sou'west smoke obscures the sunny charts,
how gulls cry on a numberless black spar.
Where North is West of North, not true, he pilots

best who feels the coast for standpipe, spire,
tower, or stack, who owns local knowledge of shoal
or ledge, whose salt nose smells the spruce shore.

Where echoes drift, where the blind groundswell
clangs an iron bell, his fish-hook hand
keeps steady on the helm. He weathers rainsquall,

linestorm, fear, who bears away from the sound
of sirens wooing him to the cape's safe lee.
He knows the ghostship bow, the sudden headland

immanent in fog; but where rocks wander, he
steers down the channel that his courage
dredges. He knows the chart is not the sea.

THE SEINERS

On the summer's end edge
of dark, the coast we seine
lies calm as after love.
The long wreck, the ledge,
float like rockweed in
the floodtide moon. The cove
is full. The milky way
drifts overhead, oars drip
light, the bow wave burns,
and herring fire the sea.

At the porpoise chase, they flip
and churn. The school turns,
and I pull a port oar
to follow, swinging the thin
pole deep, sounding to feel
their strike toward shore,
ready now to set twine
where they hang and wheel.
Girl, before we close
them off, look down once
at the swimming light
we have to love or lose.

September phosphorescence
fills the sea. The night
is round, and we row on

the surface of our dreams.
An ebbtide catch is chance,
but there! there! look down:
under us the cold light streams
ashore, and the seas dance.
Before we drift asleep,
see, love, how stars run deep.

Between their sandspit ends
we rowed, two spruce islands
moored in a blue Maine bay.
And under the Sou'west sky
we rowed ashore to swim
for love, a summer whim
when our limbs were all July.

Riding in on the tide
with shipped oars, jade
shallows under us, we
both looked down at the play
of sun on seaweed gardens,
swaying whorls in the currents
we neither could see.

And then the kelp-grown slope
slid up to meet us, steep
as a hill below our hull:
sand, stone, and clamshell
dredged by waves, time-
shaped by tide and fathom,
and then the tide was full.

We floated on hope at flood,
and over, over, the tide-
sunk bar; there where the run

of current, the waving sun,
showed clear on the waterglass
sand, on the seawind grass,
how the islands were one.

ADAM

I take thee now to be no other
than you are. In the raw weather
of Northeast storms, in summer meadows
run with only the seabirds' shadows,

I risk my naked and imperfect praise.
From noon to sunlit moon, the days
make ceremony of my quick desire.
Wave by wave, the gray stone shore

diminishes to sand, the known coast
ebbs: and we stand watching, crest
on blue and whitecap crest, who search
still for a tidal lovers' beach.

Yet never do quivering lovers touch
the secret place they join to reach;
at flood between them, love divides,
as barred islands by spring tides.

So must we, Eve, content ourselves
how close we came. At equinox, our lives
are time enough to love again,
between the loon call and the rain.

And there is world enough. I claim
this coast by giving it a name;
I give you this calm morning
as the first, without storm warning

in the cirrus sky. Fish and seal,
crab and beach-pea, breed original
in my mind: heather, starfish forms,
are mine. I love you by the terms

I make to give you. I wake to call
the osprey, tern, the slow-winged gull,
say all the sea's grave names, and build
with words this beach that is the world.

Blind lovers on the sand,
we lie apart to bathe
in sun, hand touching hand
beneath the breaking wave

of summer. We drowse, drown,
under the sun's noon weight,
breathing the sea, prone
to death, our eyelids tight

against the swimming world
of infinite light. The sky
kaleidoscopes to gold
in my spectrum-heavy eye,

brightens, fades, and grays
beneath the heatwave cloud
where we wake, castaways,
cold as the sea is loud.

THE MARGIN

Where, cast away, I wake from numb surprise
to map the island that my doubts surround,
a chance perfection makes my wonder wise.

The surf churns still, but a long perspective lies
beyond the breakers, calm and finally round
where, cast away, I wake from numb surprise.

Questioning long silence, I learn to prize
a rock pool that the thousand tides have ground;
a chance perfection makes my wonder wise.

Survivors too, plovers with piping cries
dip down to that green pool my salt hands sound
where, cast away, I wake from numb surprise.

Fed by a small sea fed by the great sea's rise,
I salvage the design by which I'm bound;
a chance perfection makes my wonder wise.

I find myself as I first colonize
the margin where original order's found:
where, cast away, I wake from numb surprise,
a chance perfection makes my wonder wise.

Lie back, daughter, let your head
be tipped back in the cup of my hand.
Gently, and I will hold you. Spread
your arms wide, lie out on the stream
and look high at the gulls. A dead-
man's-float is face down. You will dive
and swim soon enough where this tidewater
ebbs to the sea. Daughter, believe
me, when you tire on the long thrash
to your island, lie up, and survive.
As you float now, where I held you
and let go, remember when fear
cramps your heart what I told you:
lie gently and wide to the light-year
stars, lie back, and the sea will hold you.

III

HERON

In the copper marsh
I saw a stilted heron
wade the tidal wash

and I, who caught no fish,
thought the grass barren
and that jade inlet harsh

until the quick-billed splash
of the long-necked heron
fulfilled my hunter's wish.

Then in the rising rush
of those great wings, far on
I saw the herring flash

and drop. And the dash
of lesser wings in the barren
marsh flew through my flesh.

Big Dog,
my God what I cannot know,
and you by God will never learn:

Eighteen feet straight down out the barn;
not a fall, a leap! And the aching wait
while you pawed the empty air for ground
that wasn't there, and hit . . .

(Big Dog, your jaw a bloody plow)

And I stumbled below to find you swaying
on those great paws, to praise your head
in my cradled knees, and to steady, steady,
that strange dog mind.

(Big Dog, whose size and run are wolf)

It would have broken ten men in two, but you
—whose wet tongue would, had I fallen,
have done what I could not do—you lie whole,
asleep in quivering dream of the slow sheep
you herd to barn.

Big Dog
in off the street, at the marrow
may all your stolen bones be sweet.

[64]

OX-PULL: CANAAN FAIR

Old before Odysseus failed to plow his son,
great-flanked oxen knew the drag, the burden
man devised beyond his strength to pull.
Now lever, wheel, and piston make a spectacle
of strength, but still the heave of shoulder,
haul of yoke, drag slabbed granite older
than Egypt, dredging a stone-sled up
through Europe to this new country fair.
And under ox-blood maple-turn, the herd whip
spins a locust song in the Indian Summer air.

Unseasonable
as bees in April,
rime in May,
or Orion high
in June,
      days lost
somewhere in August,
green days, dun,
return at noon
as numb-winged wasps
swim in the lapse
of weather:
        sun
and weathervane
are still; the cows
wait, hillside crows
caw down to barn
the first-frost burn
of sumac, maple,
and sideyard apple.

The sky is halo-
hazed, barn and silo
smell of baled hay,
corn-crib, and dry
harvest days;

[66]

days,
goldenrod days:
and the dazzled wasps
climb numb in the lapse
of weather, lost
in what cannot last,
wings struck dumb,
in this other summer,
summer twice come.

CROSSING

STOP   LOOK   LISTEN
as gate stripes swing down,
count the cars hauling distance
upgrade through town:
warning whistle, bellclang,
engine eating steam,
engineer waving,
a fast-freight dream:
B&M boxcar,
boxcar again,
Frisco gondola,
eight-nine-ten,
Erie and Wabash,
Seaboard, U.P.,
Pennsy tankcar,
twenty-two, three,
Phoebe Snow, B&O,
thirty-four, five,
Santa Fe cattle
shipped alive,
red cars, yellow cars,
orange cars, black,
Youngstown steel
down to Mobile
on Rock Island track,
fifty-nine, sixty,
hoppers of coke,

[68]

Anaconda copper,
hotbox smoke,
eighty-eight,
red-ball freight,
Rio Grande,
Nickel Plate,
Hiawatha,
Lackawanna,
rolling fast
and loose,
ninety-seven,
coal car,
boxcar,
CABOOSE!

POLARIS

The night my fever broke
I sweat ten dreams of death,
but one dream other woke
my blood: my driven breath
like rainsqualls in my mouth
blew out and swung, force five,
steady from the South.
I dreamed I was alive

the night the weather broke,
the night we lay hove to
against the gale that woke
us into love. Back through
that morning where the mast
whipped, drumming on the hum
of shrouds, I sailed the last
of my delirium.

The night my fever broke
I hung in irons, blown far
off course. I swung and woke,
not to choose a star,
but to be compassed—full
and by—in your sure sight;
our weather turned, the pole-
star like a masthead light.

RAKER

Now all the Fall is haze,
bittersweet with smoke
these elegiac days:
the raker leans on rake,
kneedeep in leaves gone bronze
and copper and dry browns;
he scuffs a golden wake
on lawn, his curbside blaze
both funeral pyre and fire
of his unspoken praise.

Parked hard against the cornfield slant
in high Vermont, a hundred cars
(stuck at random on some last picnic)
rust in the thin winter sunset. A bent
green schoolbus, trucks without tires,
cars without wheels, are herded thick

as guernseys, ranked one way toward dusk.
Half-ton Ford and stripped Chevrolet
have come home, low in the frozen corn.
Two junked wreckers, beyond the risk
of pot-holes or insurance, lie
tipped against the silver barn.

Torn fenders, frames beyond salvage,
line the pigpen. A white gelding
nibbles downhill, too swayback to swap.
One old man feeds on this silage
of short days. Six crows, holding
altitude, circle his final crop.

RED BRICK

Behind red brick, blank windows, they stare
toward their thighs. At night a meshed moon
patrols the long wards, a bauble of terror
bounds down drugged sleep, and the forgotten
dogs bay. Coupled in childless dreams,
the suburbs under this common hill lie deaf,
while maimed innocence paws the window frames.
Some are incoherent at dawn, most are safe.
Some must be fed, immersed in the violent water
they walk; some crouch in the morning shadows
tame as hounds. Hunched cold beyond the chatter
of traffic, the tittering birds, they stare at windows
gauged by the state that loses them. Outside,
the one tall chimney of institutional smoke
fumes thick like love, the quick commuters parade
to work, and the walls are blank red brick.

Where my struck mother stays,
she wakes to thunderstorms
of doubt. Squalls blacken
her bright-surfaced dreams,
and she stands coldly shaken,
lost in the dripping trees.

The weather shuts and opens:
horizon lightning traps
her in a quick exposure
of old fears; she trips
and rises twice unsure.
No one knows how it happens.

Where my dark mother waits
for sun, the wet slate sky
builds prison thunderheads,
and she, mired in anxiety,
must bear the drumroll nights
struck mute by what she dreads.

Her numb-mouthed silences
are desperate prayer, or else
the panic count from flash
to thunderclap. Impulse
fires her woman flesh,
and fevers her thin balances.

Miles from where my mother
falls, in that rank formal
garden that I bend
to weed, the wrens chirp normal
pleasure on the wind,
wrens scale the turning weather.

Weeds like conscience clog
my rake. My mother craves
more love than any son
can give. And I, with leaves
jammed on a sharpened tine,
sweat where my two hearts tug.

Dreams from her, I wake
beyond my mother's hope
and will. Beyond the son
I was, and the thunder's shape,
I clear the overgrown
last path my heart must rake.

DESIGN

Around the tree
they won't outgrow,

plowing with
cold feet, warm breath,

to tramp a wreath
or trace the path

of their amaze-
ment in wet snow,

my children wander
at cross-purposes,

cross-sectioning
the marvelous yard.

Lost in laughter
where they blunder

kneedeep
in geometry,

neither daughter
half supposes

that while they sleep,
the tree, the yard,

the crystal maze
of quartered ring

and staggered line,
will freeze, freeze

hard: design
within design.

TWELFTH NIGHT

At Twelfth Night twilight now
the greens burn bright: the dry-spined wreath
and bittersweet returned to frozen earth,
    Canada fir
    become the fire
that wreathes a ritual circle in the snow.

    The decorations are first
to flame: old mistletoe and holly
go up in a burst of charred berry, their holy
    roots tossed on,
    a burnt seed sown,
long after the symbol and song are lost.

    Uprooted meanings flare
like watchfires in this cold backyard.
A single star outshines the ice. Unheard,
    the Magi raise
    their prayer; a blaze
of balsam climbs the still and brittle air.

    At Twelfth Night twilight now
the tree must be the final torch,
a coronal to melt the dark; the branch
    that angels swung on,
    Christ hung on,
quick tinder lit to ebb the tidal snow.

From slow bright smoke the tree
explodes in fire-veins, star-sparks rain
like fallen Pleiades. The green grain
    burns to warn
      the burner, turn
his back on ceremonial memory.

  No god's made manifest
from this raw bush. But who will light
a legend that he will not celebrate?
    In the quick match,
      the winter watch,
the burner is both burned and blessed.

NORTH

North is weather, winter, and change:
a wind-shift, snow, and how ice ages
shape the moraine of a mountain range.

At tree line the chiseled ledges
are ragged to climb; wind-twist trees
give way to the thrust of granite ridges,

peaks reach through abrasive centuries
of rain. The worn grain, the sleet-cut,
is magnified on blue Northwest days

where rock slides, like rip-tide, break out
through these geologic seas. Time
in a country of hills is seasonal light:

alpenglow, Northern lights, and tame
in October: Orion, cold hunter of stars.
Between what will be and was, rime

whites the foothill night and flowers
the rushes stilled in black millpond ice.
The dark, the nightfall temperatures

are North, and the honk of flyway geese
high over valley sleep. The woodland
is evergreen, ground pine, spruce,

and deadwood hills at the riverbend.
Black bear and mink fish beaver streams
where moose and caribou drink: beyond

the forests there are elk. Snowstorms
breed North like arctic birds that swirl
downhill, and in a blind wind small farms

are lost. At night the close cold is still,
the tilt world returns from sun to ice.
Glazed lichen is North, and snowfall

at five below. North is where rockface
and hoarfrost are formed with double grace:
love is twice warm in a cold place.

LETTER FROM A DISTANT LAND

I, on my side, require of every writer, first or last, a simple and sincere account of his own life . . . some such account as he would send to his kindred from a distant land; for if he has lived sincerely, it must have been in a distant land to me.

—Thoreau, *Walden*

Henry, my distant kin,
                I live halfway,
halfway between an airfield and your pond,
halfway within the house I moved to buy
by borrowing. On transcendental ground,
come south from colder hills and early dusk,
we claim two acres of uneven land.
Alone now, sitting at my birch-plank desk,
I see an acre out these wide new windows:
my wife cuts brush, two small girls both risk
a foot in appletrees. Across the meadows,
the alder swamp, an ash grove not yet green,
a pair of jets outrace their double shadows.
We do not look up. A grosbeak in the pine
pecks under wing, the shy hen pheasant leaves
her nibbled sumac for our scattered grain.
With rabbits, too, we share uncertain lives;
not quiet or desperate, we measure man
by how he lives and what he most believes.
I am half teacher, half-week chopping blow-down
for our fire, half-time professing words
to warm new minds with what my heart has known.
My classes are good failures. Afterwards,

I change clothes, moult my partial self,
and walk completed through the open woods.
Behind the grillwork branches where I half
confess, the chapel that I most attend
is choired by migratory birds; I loaf
within the absolution of the wind.
My thought is swiftest when my feet are slow,
but far abroad I own a spendthrift mind.
My Spanish grandfather, a tall man, knew
his knighthood from a book. So, pastoral
beside a fire, do I come slowly to know
you, odd Uncle of my wakeful, still,
and secret dawns. My least experiments
with seed, like yours with a dried apple, fail:
the weeds, slugs, borers, grow as dense
as crows. I own a herd dog, but no sheep;
my cultivation is, like learning, chance.
Slack puritan I am, I let my garden shape
itself with skunks. I am halfway, I tell you;
there are midnights when I do not sleep.

The quick night-fighters' sudden thunder shakes
this house awake. I know no metaphor
for them except to say they are great sharks
with silver fins that plane the ocean air.
Propelled by jets of flame fired through their vents,
they school a noisy mile Northeast of here,
guided by blind pilots, and by governments.
A war ago, I flew myself. Now, bound
to these two acres, I owe the several debts
a lonely conscience knows. I love this land
by the salt sweat it costs to own it whole.

My birthday was a bucksaw, I still defend
the new growth with an ax; the trees I fell
need cutting to let the hardwood grow. I chop
at the lush swamp, hack down the summer jungle
rich with flies. You know how fires earned chip
by chip are warmest. Still, you could not guess
the shapes of proved destruction. Chain saws rape
a virgin stand to stumps. Raw foremen boss
more horsepower in a fleet of airfield trucks
than Concord ever stabled. Machines as murderous
as mad bulls gore the land. Where stacked cornshocks
stood last fall, an orange oil tank flaws
the spring; girders bloom with concrete blocks.
So far, your Concord has seen four more wars.
Vegetables are high. The streets are filled
with tourists. Cheap people in expensive cars
patrol the Sunday roads. An acre sold
in 1849 sells now two hundred times
the price. Lexington is houses sprawled
on desert-dusty streets with fertile names.
The arrogant inherit lust. Everywhere,
thick rows of sportsmen fish polluted streams,
or hunt the posted woods of their own fear.
Overhead, the tight-paired jets write
cryptic warnings on the thin blue air.

Too close to earth to show to those who scan
the sky for enemy, I walked last week
beyond the impulse caught on any radar screen.
In windworn March, halfway to dawn, I woke
to feel the growing day: the wind light North-
north-west, the morning luminous, a streak

of cloud between the sunward-turning earth
and yesterday's last stars. A rebel drummer
called me like the crows. The cross-lots path
I walked was wet with melting frost, a rumor
of frogs thawed the swamp, and toward town
I heard the hard first whack of a hammer.
A casual pilgrim to the phoebe's tune,
I whistled down the distant land where you
(this same month's end) tramped out to cut white pine
with Alcott's borrowed ax. Your Walden, now,
is still half yours: a summer swimmers' beach
corrupts the eastern bank, the sun-up view,
but you, who would be saint in a formal church,
are honored still on the farther shores, preserved
in the commonwealth of hemlock, elm, and birch.
Your hut is marked by stone, the pond was saved
by taxes for a public park. Emerson's
strict laws of compensation have reserved
a parking space for Sunday lovers: beer cans
drift where you knelt soberly to drink,
and small boys smoke like truant puritans.
Such is August on the swimmers' bank,
but not my sharp March dawn. Between ice-out
and spring, I walk in time to hear the honk
of two stray geese, the song of a white-throat
soloing after his mate in your celibate woods.
It is the same, I tell you. Shadowy trout
rise like the swift perfection of your words,
the backyard journal of your human praise
is proved in the red oaks' blood-dark buds.
I like to think how animals would freeze
to see your stick, your crooked genius, poke

[85]

the leafy underbrush; until you froze
yourself, and all the thicket woodcock, duck,
and small scared beasts of Walden's shore
turned curious. Here, between the dark
and sudden milktrain day, halfway from fear,
halfway to spring, I say these natural names
to honor you as poet of the turning year.
Beside the ministry of waves, the times
of men are seasons, windfall seeds that spill
toward fruit: the perfect globe or wormy shames
of Adam. All poets climb back Eden's hill
within their own backyard. Woods and pond
were your recovery of the crop that's possible,
a harvest of good words grown from the land
that brings the whole world home. I cultivate
a different orchard, pruning under the sound
of probable war. The day's first silver jet
reflects first sunlight where I turn away
from Walden, turn, stop, look back, and start
again. Up the bank, I cross the highway
where a skunk got lost in headlights: traffic-
flat, his flowering intestines lie halfway
in sun. This new March day is sweetened thick
with death. But when was any season less?
You felt the cold fall snap of John Brown's neck,
owned a winter conscience, smelled slavery's grass-
fire torch the long dry land to civil war,
from Bull Run to Savannah to the Wilderness.
I tell you, Henry, distant as we are,
the good, the brave, are no more a majority
than when you walked this far spring shore.
Man, by his human nature, is not free,

but where his wildness is alive to swamp
and hill, he learns to live most naturally.
Still, a saunterer must make his camp
in strange unholy lands, begging alms
and passage for belief. I take no stump
except for liberty to listen to the elms,
to walk the cold wood, to sleep on bedrock
thought, and to say my winter psalms.
A century from where your wisdom struck
its temporary camp, I cross the middleground
toward truth. At home beneath both oak
and jet, praising what I halfway understand,
I walk this good March morning out
to say my strange love in a distant land.